6 **JOHN QUINCY ADAMS** 1825–29	7 **ANDREW JACKSON** 1829–37	8 **MARTIN VAN BUREN** 1837–41	9 **WILLIAM HENRY HARRISON** 1841	**JOHN TYLER** 1841–45
16 **ABRAHAM LINCOLN** 1861–65	17 **ANDREW JOHNSON** 1865–69	18 **ULYSSES S. GRANT** 1869–77	19 **RUTHERFORD B. HAYES** 1877–81	20 **JAMES A. GARFIELD** 1881
27 **WILLIAM HOWARD TAFT** 1909–13	28 **WOODROW WILSON** 1913–21	29 **WARREN G. HARDING** 1921–23	30 **CALVIN COOLIDGE** 1923–29	31 **HERBERT HOOVER** 1929–33
37 **RICHARD M. NIXON** 1969–74	38 **GERALD R. FORD** 1974–77	39 **JIMMY CARTER** 1977–81	40 **RONALD REAGAN** 1981–89	41 **GEORGE H. W. BUSH** 1989–93

THE WHITE HOUSE HAS BEEN THE HOME
AND OFFICE OF EVERY PRESIDENT OF THE
UNITED STATES SINCE JOHN ADAMS.

Rocco at the White House Easter Egg Roll!

Text by Rocco Smirne • Illustrated by John Hutton

THE WHITE HOUSE HISTORICAL ASSOCIATION

Introduction

The Easter Egg Roll is one of the many special ways that the president and first lady welcome children to the White House. It is among the oldest of annual events, and it is probably the most fun. Thousands of children and their families fill the president's backyard on Easter Monday as they enjoy rolling eggs, listening to the music of the Marine Band, taking drawing lessons, decorating cookies, and gathering around as authors read their books aloud. Rocco Smirne is just eight years old, but he knows much about the White House and has attended many Easter Egg Rolls. He wrote this book to let you know what to expect if you visit and also how to create some of the same activities in your own home that kids enjoy at the White House. Rain or shine, Rocco knows how to have fun, and he wants you to join him!

Stewart D. McLaurin
President, White House Historical Association

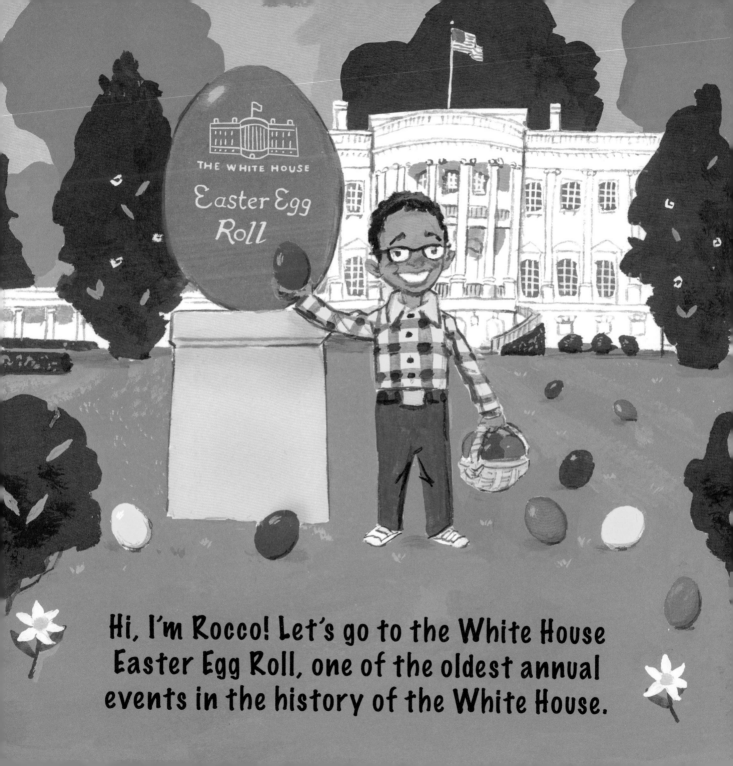

Hi, I'm Rocco! Let's go to the White House Easter Egg Roll, one of the oldest annual events in the history of the White House.

The Easter Egg Roll takes place on the White House Grounds. That's the president's backyard!

Children were first welcomed to roll their Easter Eggs at the White House by President Rutherford B. Hayes in 1878!

Today, thousands of children are welcomed for fun at an Egg Roll at the White House on the Monday after Easter—that is, Easter Monday!

There are many fun activities to try at the Easter
Egg Roll—including games, music, art, and more!
Here I am exploring the festivities with my friends.

The Egg Roll is my favorite activity! I hope you can go to the White House, too, but, if not, you can roll eggs—plastic, wooden, or hard-boiled eggs—at home! To roll an egg, get a wooden spoon, bend over to reach the egg, push it along with your spoon, and go as fast as you can to the finish!

At the White House, children decorate Easter cookies. You can do this at home with store bought cookies or ones you made yourself. My favorite toppings are sprinkles and icing. Be creative! Decorating cookies is fun, but the best part is eating them!

Sugar Cookies

2 sticks butter, soft
¾ cup sugar
1 tsp vanilla extract

1 egg
3 cups all-purpose flour
¼ tsp salt

1. Cream butter and sugar until smooth—by hand with a spatula or using an electric mixer.

2. Stir in vanilla extract.

3. Beat egg in a separate bowl. Then stir into butter and sugar mixture.

4. In a separate bowl, stir salt into flour. Then slowly add flour mixture into the butter and sugar mixture until fully combined.

5. Divide the dough in two. Shape each piece into a flat, round disk.

6. Wrap each disk in plastic and chill in refrigerator for at least 1 hour or until firm.

7. Roll chilled dough to ¼ inch thick.

8. Dip cookie cutter into flour and cut cookie shapes (dip for each cut).

9. Put cookies on cookie sheet lined with parchment paper.

10. Bake cookies in a preheated oven at 350 degrees for 10-12 minutes, until light brown.

11. Let cookies cool on cookie sheet before removing them.

12. Decorate the cookies with sprinkles and icing.

At the White House kids can look for eggs hidden in straw. It is called an Egg Hunt, and you can do it at home, too! Have someone hide colored eggs in your house or backyard. Then look for them. Their bright colors might give them away.

If you have an Egg Hunt at home you could
even have a competition with your family and
friends to see who can find the most eggs.

At the White House Easter Egg Roll,
the Marine Band plays music all day!
My favorite musician is the drummer.

Rain or shine, the Egg Roll is always fun. I have the most fun in the rain! Make sure to be prepared!

Be sure to stop by the reading nook! This is a special place at the White House Egg Roll for authors to read their books. My mom and I read the book I wrote about traveling with the presidents!

Sometimes authors even sign their books at special tables. I signed my book in the White House Visitor Center. You can use your imagination to write stories, too!

Artist John Hutton made the pictures in my books.
He often gives drawing lessons at the Egg Roll.
Here are some of his lessons for you to try at home.

Follow these instructions to prepare for your drawing lessons:

1. Get paper and something to draw with, such as a pencil, marker, or crayon—whichever might be your favorite!

2. Copy the step-by-step examples on each page to complete your own drawing.

3. Make sure to sign your name on your new artwork!

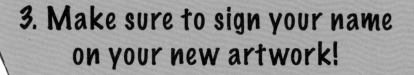

Draw an Easter Egg!

1.

2.

3.

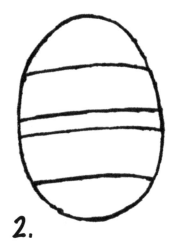

4.

Draw the Easter Bunny!

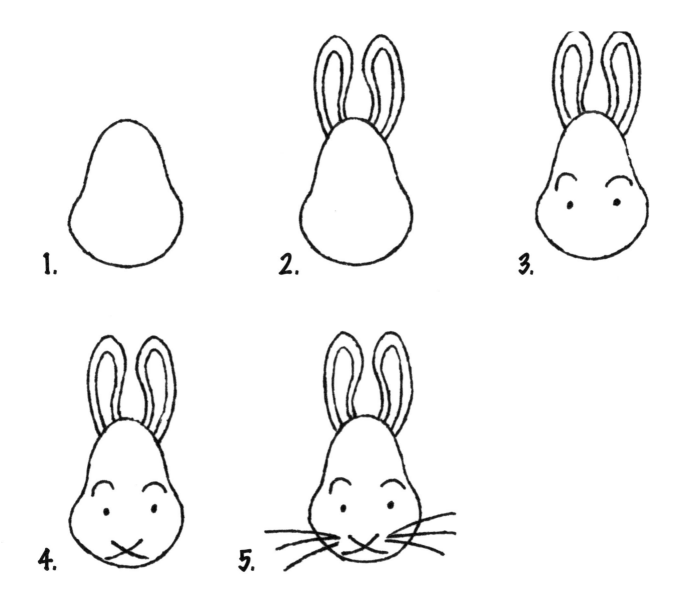

1.

2.

3.

4.

5.

Draw the Marine Band drummer!

1.   2.   3.   4.

Draw the White House!

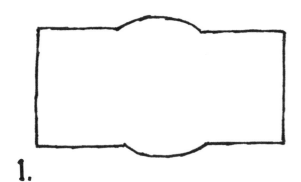

1.

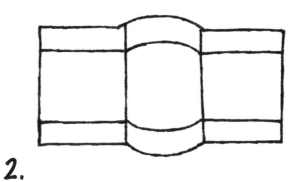

2.

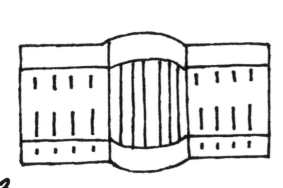

3.

4.

I hope you enjoyed the Easter Egg Roll! Be sure to keep reading to learn even more about the White House!

About the Author

Rocco Smirne attends elementary school in Fairfax County, Virginia. He enjoys attending festivals, parades, and activities in the Nation's Capital. When not out exploring, Rocco enjoys reading, drawing, and video games. Rocco is co-author of *A White House Alphabet* and author of *Rocco Travels with the Presidents!*.

About the Illustrator

John Hutton is a professor of art history at Salem College, where he has taught since 1990. He is the author of *How to Draw the Presidents* and has illustrated many children's books. He lives in Winston-Salem, North Carolina.

THE WHITE HOUSE HISTORICAL ASSOCIATION is a nonprofit educational organization, founded in 1961 for the purpose of enhancing the understanding, appreciation, and enjoyment of the Executive Mansion. All proceeds from the sale of the Association's books and products are used to fund the acquisition of historic furnishings and artwork for the permanent White House Collection, assist in the preservation of public rooms, and further its educational mission.

Chief Publishing Officer: Marcia Mallet Anderson; Associate Vice President of Publishing: Lauren McGwin; Senior Editorial and Production Manager: Kristen Hunter Mason; Editorial and Production Manager: Margaret Strolle; Editorial Coordinator: Rebecca Durgin Kerr; Consulting Editor: Ann Hofstra Grogg

Original drawings by John Hutton are dedicated by the artist to James and Susan Hutton.
Copyright © 2023 by the White House Historical Association

10 9 8 7 6 5 4 3 2 1   Library of Congress Control Number: 2023930384   ISBN 978-1-950273-39-3   Printed in Italy

1 GEORGE WASHINGTON 1789–97	**2** JOHN ADAMS 1797–1801	**3** THOMAS JEFFERSON 1801–09	**4** JAMES MADISON 1809–17	**5** JAMES MONROE 1817–25
11 JAMES K. POLK 1845–49	**12** ZACHARY TAYLOR 1849–50	**13** MILLARD FILLMORE 1850–53	**14** FRANKLIN PIERCE 1853–57	**15** JAMES BUCHANAN 1857–61
21 CHESTER A. ARTHUR 1881–85	**22 & 24** GROVER CLEVELAND 1885–89, 1893–97	**23** BENJAMIN HARRISON 1889–93	**25** WILLIAM McKINLEY 1897–1901	**26** THEODORE ROOSEVELT 1901–09
32 FRANKLIN D. ROOSEVELT 1933–45	**33** HARRY S. TRUMAN 1945–53	**34** DWIGHT D. EISENHOWER 1953–61	**35** JOHN F. KENNEDY 1961–63	**36** LYNDON B. JOHNSON 1963–69
42 WILLIAM J. CLINTON 1993–2001	**43** GEORGE W. BUSH 2001–09	**44** BARACK OBAMA 2009–17	**45** DONALD J. TRUMP 2017–2021	**46** JOSEPH R. BIDEN 2021–